# THE SCIENCE OF
# TRACK AND FIELD

By
## Emilie Dufresne

PLAY
SMART

Published in 2021 by
**KidHaven Publishing, an Imprint of Greenhaven Publishing, LLC**
353 3rd Avenue
Suite 255
New York, NY 10010

© 2021 Booklife Publishing
This edition is published by arrangement with Booklife Publishing

Cataloging-in-Publication Data

Names: Dufresne, Emilie.
Title: The science of track and field / Emilie Dufresne.
Description: New York : KidHaven Publishing, 2021. | Series: Play
smart | Includes glossary and index.
Identifiers: ISBN 9781534535800 (pbk.) | ISBN 9781534535824
(library bound) | ISBN 9781534535817 (6 pack) | ISBN 9781534535831
(ebook)
Subjects: LCSH: Track and field--Juvenile literature. | Sports sciences-
-Juvenile literature.
Classification: LCC GV557.D847 2021 | DDC 796.42--dc23

Printed in the United States of America

CPSIA compliance information: Batch #BS20K: For further information contact
Greenhaven Publishing LLC, New York, New York, at 1-844-317-7404.

Please visit our website, www.greenhavenpublishing.com.
For a free color catalog of all our high-quality books,
call toll free 1-844-317-7404 or fax 1-844-317-7405.

Find us on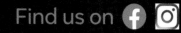

**Photo credits:**

Cover – JaySi, nampix, max blain, Papa Annur, Inked Pixels, WoodysPhotos. 2 - benedix. 4 - CAT SCAPE. 5 - Lapina. 6 - Dmitry
Sheremeta.7 - Dmitry Sheremeta. 8 - ostill. 9 - wavebreakmedia. 10 - Denis Kuvaev. 12 - Vectorfusionart. 13 - wavebreakmedia.
14 - ostill. 15 - sirtravelalot. 16 - Petrovic Igor. 17 - ostill. 18 - sportpoint. 19 - sirtravelalot. 20 - sportpoint. 21 - StockphotoVideo. 22 -
VGstockstudio, pattang, TinnaPong. 23 - Sergey Novikov.

Images are courtesy of Shutterstock.com. With thanks to Getty Images, Thinkstock Photo, and iStockphoto.

All facts, statistics, web addresses, and URLs in this book were verified as valid and accurate at time of writing.
No responsibility for any changes to external websites or references can be accepted by either the author or publisher.

# CONTENTS

Words that look like **this** can be found in the glossary on page 24.

# ON YOUR MARK

Are you ready to find out about the patterns, **forces**, and angles at work in track and field? Then put on your running shoes. It's time to warm up!

**ARE YOU READY?**
**THEN GET SET; LET'S GO!**

There are lots of different track and field events. They include running short and long distances, throwing different objects, and jumping in different ways.

# AND THEY'RE OFF!

You can use starting blocks at the beginning of a sprint. This will give you something to push off from. The friction between your shoes and the blocks will stop you from sliding backward.

**FOOT PUSHES OFF**

Friction is a force between two objects moving against each other. It's hard to rub your socks on the carpet, isn't it? That's friction at work!

**BLOCK STOPS ANY SLIDING**

**130 DEGREES**

**90 DEGREES**

Angles are also important when using starting blocks. When in the "get set" position, your **dominant** leg should be at a right angle, or 90 degrees. Your other leg should be at a larger angle, around 130 degrees.

# HOW TO HURDLE

**FORWARD MOMENTUM**

Pushing forward before and after each hurdle will give you good forward **momentum**.

Hurdling is all about keeping your momentum when jumping over the hurdles. Momentum is made up of your speed and **mass**. Slowing down to jump the hurdles will mean you have less momentum.

It's also important to know how many steps you run between each hurdle. This will help you have a running and jumping pattern. Lots of people do three steps between each jump.

You can run as fast as you can to build up momentum, knowing you still have time to jump.

JUMP!

STEP 3    STEP 2    STEP 1

# SHOT PUT SHOWDOWN

The shot is a very heavy ball. You push, or put, it hard into the air, so it lands as far away as possible. There are lots of different forces that affect a shot put.

WHEN THE SHOT IS PUSHED, IT HAS BOTH FORWARD AND UPWARD FORCE.

Other forces are also acting on the shot put, such as air resistance and gravity.

AIR RESISTANCE AND GRAVITY EVENTUALLY MAKE THE BALL FALL TO THE GROUND.

THE HARDER YOU PUSH THE BALL, THE FARTHER IT WILL GO.

Air resistance is when the air pushes back against a moving object.

Gravity is the force that pulls everything toward the center of Earth.

# DARE TO DISCUS

The discus is a round disk that has to be thrown into the air spinning. If thrown at an upward angle, it can create upward lift.

The angle you throw it at is called the angle of attack.

**32 TO 37 DEGREES**

**THE BEST ANGLE OF ATTACK IS 32 TO 37 DEGREES.**

The air moves faster over the curved top of the discus. The air below the discus has a higher **pressure**. This lifts the discus higher into the air.

LOW PRESSURE

LIFT

HIGH PRESSURE

With a good angle of attack, you will get good lift, and your discus will travel higher and farther.

# THROW THROUGH THE TIP

When throwing a javelin, the correct angle will help you to get the best distance. Always get a good run-up before throwing your javelin to get good forward momentum.

**JAVELIN LINE**

As you are about to throw it, hold the javelin in line with your eyes.

Throwing through the tip means that your hand should follow the angle that you want the javelin to be thrown at. The best angle to throw a javelin at is 45 degrees.

**45 DEGREES**

**ARM ROTATION**

# LANDING THE LONG JUMP

Landing the perfect long jump is all about the shapes you make when you are in the air. Making the right shapes will help you jump farther.

WHEN YOU FIRST JUMP, JUMP UPWARD AND KEEP YOUR BODY STRAIGHT LIKE A RECTANGLE.

PULL YOUR ARMS UP AND OVER YOUR HEAD AND TUCK YOUR LEGS INTO YOUR CHEST. THEN PUSH YOUR ARMS AND LEGS STRAIGHT OUT IN FRONT OF YOU AND FOLD INTO A TRIANGLE.

ONCE YOU HAVE GOTTEN AS HIGH AS YOU CAN, START TO PULL YOUR LEGS AND ARMS BACKWARD INTO A SEMICIRCLE SHAPE.

# THE FOSBURY FLOP

The Fosbury flop is a **technique** used in the high jump. When you jump, you turn your body to face the sky and bend your back around and over the pole.

FACE THE SKY. ↑

BEND BODY
AROUND POLE.

The Fosbury flop is easier than jumping over the bar like a hurdle. This is because of centers of gravity. Your center of gravity is where your weight is **concentrated**.

The Fosbury flop keeps your center of gravity as low as possible. This means less energy is needed to push you over the bar.

WHEN STANDING UP, YOUR CENTER OF GRAVITY IS NEAR YOUR BELLY BUTTON.

# THE PERFECT POLE VAULT

The perfect pole vault is a mix of energy **transfer** and angles. When you are running up, you build up lots of energy.

## THE ENERGY IS NOW IN THE POLE.

When the pole is pushed into the ground, the energy is transferred to it.

**90 DEGREES**

Hold on to the pole tightly, and the energy stored in the pole will push you upward and over the bar.

Once the pole reaches a 90-degree angle, even more energy is stored in it. The more energy that is stored in the pole, the easier it will be to get over the bar.

# SEE THE SCIENCE

If you don't have starting blocks, you can use a wall to push off from. Let's try an experiment. To see the science in action, you will need:

**A TAPE MEASURE**

**A FRIEND AND A WALL**

**A STOPWATCH**

# METHOD

1. MEASURE A DISTANCE OF 20 METERS.
2. RUN THE DISTANCE WITHOUT USING THE WALL TO PUSH OFF FROM.
3. DON'T FORGET TO TIME IT! WRITE DOWN HOW LONG IT TOOK.
4. NOW RUN USING THE WALL TO PUSH OFF FROM AT THE START.
5. DON'T FORGET TO MAKE SURE YOUR LEGS ARE AT THE CORRECT ANGLES!
6. HOW LONG DID IT TAKE THIS TIME? WAS IT ANY QUICKER?
7. NOW SWAP AND TIME YOUR FRIEND.

# GLOSSARY

| | |
|---|---|
| **concentrated** | having a lot of something in one place |
| **dominant** | most important or strongest |
| **forces** | pushes or pulls on an object |
| **mass** | how much matter a body or object has |
| **momentum** | the force an object has when it moves, based on its speed and mass |
| **pressure** | a force that is caused by something pushing on something else |
| **technique** | a way of doing something |
| **transfer** | to pass on from one thing to another |

# INDEX